COWBOYS

John Eggen

4880 Lower Valley Road, Atglen, PA 19310 USA

In Appreciation

To my wife Marjorie for her help in putting this book together;

To Byron Sherman, nephew of the photographer who gave me so much information;

To William Blanton, a Colorado rancher who made sure that all the information and statements on ranching were correct;

To Mary M. Davis, Library Assistant in the Pikes Peak Library District for her valuable assistance;

To Loren R. Whittmore, author of An Illustrated History of Ranching in the Pikes Peak Region*;*

To Ralph C. Taylor, author of Colorado South of the Border.

Copyright © 1992 by John Eggen
Library of Congress Catalog Number: 92-60639

ISBN: 0-88740-436-7
Printed in China

Published by Schiffer Publishing Ltd.
4880 Lower Valley Road
Atglen, PA 19310
Phone: (610) 593-1777; Fax: (610) 593-2002
E-mail: Info@schifferbooks.com
Please visit our web site catalog at
www.schifferbooks.com

Autographed copies of the book are available from the author. Also, prints made from the original glass negatives are available by writing to John E. Eggen—Box 55, Lebanon, Oregon 97355

Contents

Frank Sherman: The Photographer

Frank M. Sherman's tombstone in the Powel Cemetery near Lebanon, Oregon.

It was in the spring of 1903 that Frank Sherman, who had a photography studio and souvenir shop in Colorado Springs, decided that he should have more post cards to sell. Frank had three brothers who worked for the Holt Livestock Co. in Hugo, Colorado. Seeing their life as an excellent source for photographs for post cards, set out to travel with the cowboys on their spring roundup to take photographs of their work on the open range.

Frank arrived in Hugo, Colorado with his camera equipment, consisting of a 5 x 7 view camera and tripod, a black focusing cloth and plenty of 5 x 7 glass negatives.

His brother Stanford was assembling the men and equipment for the roundup when he received a telegram telling him to wait because President Roosevelt was coming through Hugo on the train. This gave Frank Sherman the opportunity to photograph "Teddy Roosevelt and the Hugo Cowboys," a small booklet assembled by the photographer and offered for sale.

The Holt Ranch covered a very large area of owned and leased land as well as extensive areas of open range. Frank was able to take a great variety of photographs there and at other ranches. It is not known how much time Frank spent taking photographs of the cowboys, however it is known that he was in Rocky Ford for the "Watermelon Picnic" in August and probably was there for the fall roundup.

In 1906 his doctor advised Frank to move to a lower altitude for his health. Frank had a friend in Lebanon, Oregon, so he went there, taking the boxes of negatives with him. He bought property about two miles from Lebanon, close to the Santiam River. In 1911 Frank married Hallie Umenhoffer, a widow with two children. They had a son in 1912.

It was reported that Frank Sherman for many years had been one of the most prominent small fruit growers in the Lebanon, Oregon area and had made many exhibits at the state fair, where he won prizes for his exhibits. He also conducted the Linn County Exhibit at the fair and had charge of the Community Exhibit of Lebanon, which won first prize at the Linn County Fair in 1921.

In November, 1921, the river flooded and water came up around the house, causing the corner to settle. The following March a neighbor was helping Frank level up the house and they found there were many rats living under the house. Frank spread a line of corn on the ground and several rats came out and were eating the corn. Frank was able to kill them all with one shot of a shotgun. He then laid the shotgun down and went in the house to see if the floor was level. He came out and picked up the shotgun by the barrel. It was an old gun and very undependable. When he picked it up it fired, hitting him in the

*Frank M. Sherman, the wonderful photographer who took these beautiful photographs of the cowboys'
life in 1903. He used glass plates, making it possible for me to have this book and the two former
editions for future generations to enjoy and understand the way the cowboys lived around the turn of
the century—John Eggen*

chest and killing him instantly. His widow took the children and what she wanted out of the house and moved away, later selling the house.

She had no use for the glass negatives so they were left in the house. They remained there until about 1966 when the occupant of the house called me at Eggen Photographs and asked if I wanted the boxes of glass negatives. If I didn't, she would dispose of them in the city garbage dump. I told her I would be there in a short time and take them off her hands. When I checked the negatives I found there were over three hundred 5 x 7 glass plates. It is believed to be the only collection of its kind in existence, the complete pictorial record of the cowboys on the open range around the turn of the century. In 1987, after ten years of retirement, I was urged to produce a book of photographs from the glass negatives. The West that Was, was the result. It has received excellent reviews and responses, both in the United States and Europe.

The Cowboys

It was a man's world on the ranch in those early years. The cowboy had to be tough and hard as nails.

There was a strict code of ethics among the cowboys. They would not tolerate a weakling or a complainer. No matter how badly they were injured or how much pain they were experiencing, they would not complain. They took discomfort and hardship in stride and made the best of it. The boss had to earn the respect of the men, but once he did, they would do whatever he asked of them without question.

Profanity was part of their language and the favorite expression was "son of a bitch," which referred to a man who was not liked as well as any animal or thing that earned the cowboy's wrath. However, there were individuals who would never use profanity and there were cowboys who later became religious leaders and pastors. Occasionally, there was a ranch owner who would not allow profanity and any employee using it would be fired. And of course none of the cowboys used profanity or off color language when around women.

This was a rare experience. They spent most of their lives without female companionship. During the roundup there were no women at all, and around the ranch women were only rarely seen. When they encountered a woman, cowboys tended to be shy. The only time they ever publicly touched a girl was when they were dancing, which was not often.

"Sherman Bros." Francis, Seeley, Stanford, and Frank, the photographer.

Working on a ranch was not without risks. The cowboys handled half-broke horses that could buck and kick, and handled cattle that rarely saw a man on foot. Cows became very belligerent if their calves were taken from them. Bulls could suddenly turn on a horse and rider, goring the horse and possibly breaking the rider's leg. This indeed happened to my wife when she was a young cowgirl. The horn of the bull missed her leg and gashed the side of her horse. She immediately went home where her father treated the horse's wound.

Saddle horses spooked, bucked and sometimes threw their hapless riders. Although the cowboys wore high heeled boots to prevent them from slipping through the stirrup. It was still possible. If this happened, the rider could be dragged to his death by the horse.

The weather was very changeable on the plains. It could be hot and dusty one day and cold and windy the next, and at any time there could be a sudden downpour. Other times there might be a cold drizzle lasting for many days. It was always a challenge driving the cattle into a 60 or 70 miles per hour gale. At night a sudden lightning storm always threatened to spook the cattle and start a stampede. With such changeable weather, pneumonia was always a threat and with few doctors, a man might have to ride for days to see a doctor who was often mediocre at best.

Added to these dangers and discomforts was the not so pleasant experience of sleeping on the ground. Baths were rare and when one was available, it was in a stream or pond. For all of this, the wages for cowboys were low, and they were often paid in cattle, but many cowboys started their own ranch in this way.

The Sherman Brothers. (L-R) Francis, Seeley, Frank, and Stanford.

Seeley and Frank Sherman

The Twins—Stanford and Seeley Sherman. Most of the cowboys trailing herds north from Texas and Mexico were boys in their teens. Their destinations were varied but included Colorado, Kansas, Wyoming, and Montana. It was a dangerous trip, which included hostile Indians, treacherous river crossings, barren deserts, and raging storms and stampedes. Stanford Sherman had been on these cattle drives when he was in his teens. He was roundup foreman for the Holt Cattle Co. when he was only twenty years old.

The Ranchers

Col. William Holt ranch home, Ramah, Colorado. This photograph was taken by Newton Tripp. Courtesy of Don Golding.

William T. Holt

One of the earliest men to venture out into the open ranges to develop a permanent ranch operation was William T. Holt from Portland, Maine. Holt was born in Yarmouth, Maine in 1839. He became a colonel in the army, and later took up law. In the 1860s he traveled to Colorado Springs for his health; it is reported that he suffered from asthma. Col. Holt was a newcomer with a plan to buy choice homesteads with "live" water (running water such as a stream) and he pursued his plan vigorously and paid well for what he bought. By 1877 Col. Holt was running about 8000 head of cattle. In addition to his own land, Holt was able to rent land that the railroad companies were granted in return for building the railroads and land the Federal government turned over to the state for revenue.

John D. Dickinson of Hugo, Colorado, best described the Holt Ranch operation in an article he wrote for the September, 1942 issue of Colorado Magazine. *The article was entitled "Life in Eastern Colorado," and was quoted in* An Illustrated History of Ranching in the Pikes Peak Region, *by Loren R. Whittemore.*

"On March 26, 1875, I commenced working for the William T. Holt Co., which ranched fifty miles east of Colorado Springs, running both sheep and cattle. Eastern Colorado at that time was a wide open country with no fences. Barbed wire had not come into use in this part of the country at that time. One could ride from the Holt Ranch to the Arkansas River without seeing anyone and then on into Texas."

"Very few people now living know what an old time roundup was like. A cow outfit would consist of a mess wagon to carry the bed and food, a cook, about eight riders...and a horse herder. The outfit would start to work about May 1st down in Kansas, east of the present state line. When all the outfits got together, there would be sometimes 30 or more wagons and 200 or more riders with 500 to 800 horses. This group would include most of the cow outfits of the Divide country, those along the Arkansas River and a few from the Platte River country."

Col. Holt's death in September of 1894 was rather sudden, although for years he had suffered from asthma. Brights disease developed. W.H. Jones, manager of the Holt Co. received a message that the Colonel was seriously ill and went to see him, taking a doctor with him. Nothing could be done and he passed away at 55 years of age.

The Holt Livestock Co., continued to operate under the care of a manager. It was now owned by heirs and stockholders. In later years the ranch was built up to several thousand acres of owned land, nearly all on live water, and over 20,000 acres under lease. There were 12,000 head of cattle, 1000 horses, and 120,000 sheep.

These were truly the days of free enterprise and independence. Cowboys were known to quit one

The Field ranch.

outfit and join another because they had better "grub." With Jack Keppel as his cook, Stanford Sherman, Holt's roundup boss, had no trouble finding cowboys.

Lewis H. Field

Lewis H. Field was born in Philadelphia, Pennsylvania in November, 1854. He moved to Colorado in 1881 because of health problems. There he worked on various ranches before purchasing his own place in 1882. He did much to improve the ranch, including building the house, barn, and sheds, irrigating the property from the Rush Creek, and being the first in the area to fence his property with barbed wire.

Field was an avid sportsman and was one of a group of ranchers that formed the Shepherd's Golf Club, which required each member to maintain a nine hole course on his ranch. He was also active in politics and community affairs.

The cowboys that worked for Field were well fed, which was an important fact. Field was known as a true friend and neighbor who never interfered in anyone else's business and was always willing to help in time of need.

George W. Barker

George Watt Barker was Canadian-born. He met his wife when they were both students at the University of Colorado at Boulder. Dora Ellen Peterson was the first woman in the first graduating class. They homesteaded in Karval to raise their cattle. They built a reservoir, planted an orchard and extensive garden, and grew corn, sorghum, millets, and forage.

They also ran a dairy operation that was quite well known in the area and provided a cash "crop" of butter. Cowboys stopped for fresh buttermilk after working on the range.

Like other homesteaders, they had to do the best they could, raising ten children.

The golfers. In 1903 the ranches were few and far between. Social life was difficult. However, the ranchers did have their golf club, and to be a member the rancher had to build a golf course on his ranch. They would then take turns hosting a golf weekend. Some of the golfers had to travel for days each way, but it was a way to socialize and enjoy a weekend.

Cox Ranche.

The Barker Ranch. The house is dug into the side of a south slope to get the maximum sunshine and protection from the wind. The prevailing wind was from the northwest and if the house was on a southeast slope, it would be buried by drifted snow in the winter. A draw on the northwest of the buildings caught the snow and left the buildings relatively clear.

Teddy Roosevelt and The Hugo Cowboys

President's train is due in 5 min.

"President's train due in 5 minutes." The photographers caption says it all. This visit by Teddy Roosevelt in 1903 filled the area with excitement. Frank Sherman captured the activities on film and published a string-bound photographic account of the event. Presumably these were for sale in his studio.

It was nearly time for the spring roundup to start on the oz (Bar OZ) ranch. The roundup foreman, Stanford Sherman, was in Hugo, Colorado to assemble a large crew, plus a chuck wagon and a cook for the roundup of about 12,000 head of cattle. Stanford Sherman, his twin brother Seeley, and older brother Francis worked for the Holt Cattle Co., which owned the Bar OZ. Another brother, Frank, who owned a photographic studio in Colorado Springs, had come to Hugo to take photographs of the roundup.

Stanford and the crew were ready to leave when he received a telegram that he was to wait. President Teddy Roosevelt would be coming through Hugo on the train on the morning of May 3rd.

The round up crew decided to have a chuckwagon breakfast ready for Teddy. The chuckwagon was set up by the railroad tracks and Jack Keppel, the cook, prepared the breakfast. Al Brookway rode out and met the train about a mile out of town and invited the President for breakfast. Teddy thanked him for the invitation, but said he couldn't make it. His schedule was too tight. He would, however, have the train stop so he could wave to the crowd.

The train stopped and Teddy smelled Jack Keppel's dutch oven cooking and said, "Hell, boys I got to have some of that chuck." He did and Frank Sherman was there to take photographs.

The photographs of Teddy Roosevelt at breakfast are from a booklet entitled President Roosevelt and the Hugo Cowboys *produced in 1903 by Frank M. Sherman.*

Getting breakfast for Teddy.

Newspaper men.

COPYRIGHTED
-1903- BY-
F.M. SHERMAN

PRES. Roosevelt's Cowboy Breakfast

"Pres. Roosevelt's Cowboy Breakfast. Oliver Ingram, President Roosevelt, General Sherman Bell (rear), Gov. Peabody, Stanford Sherman, F.M. Sherman, photographer. Others unknown." Taken from Sherman's President Roosevelt and the Hugo Cowboys.

PRES. R. "THAT STEAK LOOKS FINE"

COPYRIGH
1903-8
F.M. SHERM

"Pres. R.: 'That steak looks fine.' John Heyman, two unknowns, Stanford Sherman, roundup foreman for Holt Co., $\overline{OZ}$, Frank Sherman (derby hat) the photographer, two unknowns. In front, President Roosevelt and Jack Keppel bending over kettles." Taken from Sherman's **President Roosevelt and the Hugo Cowboys.**

24

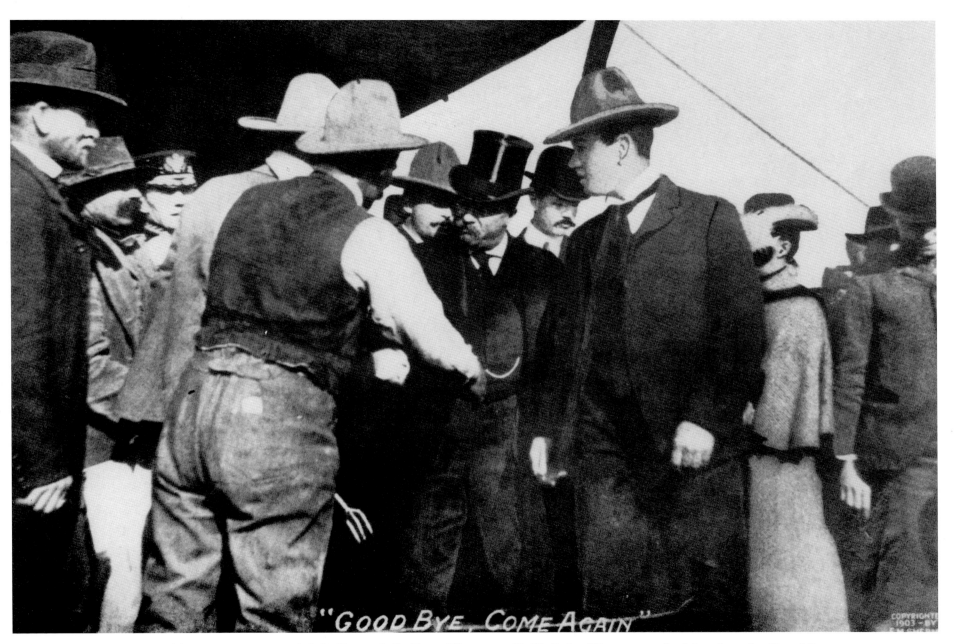

"GOOD BYE, COME AGAIN"

"'Good bye, come again.' J.O. Dostal, ?, Gen. Sherman Bell, John Heyman, shaking hands, President Roosevelt, F.M. Sherman. Others not identified." Taken from Sherman's President Roosevelt and the Hugo Cowboys.

The Cowboy's Life

The life of the cowboy was not for the timid or weak. It took a rugged individual to put up with the razzing from the other men until he proved himself capable of handling any situation. Once he gained the respect of the others, he was part of a close-knit group.

Life was not easy on the roundups, sleeping in a bedroll on the hard ground, up at dawn. There were no toilet facilities. They just did whatever was necessary. While the crew ate breakfast, sometimes out on the ground in wind and rain, the wrangler rounded up and readied the horses for the men to saddle up as soon as breakfast was over. They might be in the saddle for the next 10 hours. They couldn't eat lunch (known as dinner) together because some of the men had to stay with the cattle. In the late afternoon the night riders ate and went out to replace the day riders who came in, took care of their horses, and then had their supper.

The night riders had a lonesome job, especially on a dark, starless night. Usually they sang or talked to themselves which helped to keep the cattle from getting spooked. It is amazing how quickly an animal can jump to its feet when suddenly surprised. As a young man on my family's ranch in South Dakota, one dark spring night, I stumbled into a two year old steer that appeared to be asleep. As I pitched forward, the animal jumped to its feet so fast that it flipped me on over and I landed on my feet, which was lucky for me since it was in the cow yard!

Ranch owners had to have a large herd of horses. At least four were needed for each rider. A horse was not ridden for more than one day at a time, then given time to rest and eat. The cowpunchers owned their saddles, but rode the ranch's horses.

It was common practice for the men to own a side arm, usually a 38, 44, or 45 caliber. In 1903, however, about the only time they wore the pistol was when hunting or when dressed up to give a macho appearance. The cowboy gunfighter or gunslinger was usually the product of western writers. But most gunslingers were, by the turn of the century, actually easterners or gangs of desperados who tried to show off their bravado with a gun; they were not cowboys. In earlier days of ranching a gun was a more important part of the cowboy's equipment due to roving bands of renegade Indians and cattle rustlers. Many of the rustlers had been in the Confederate army and came west with their guns after the Civil War was over.

There was generally a lot of rivalry between cowboys who worked for different outfits. Each claimed that they had the best ropers and the best riders and often spun yarns to make their point:

"Roll out boys"

"Roll out boys." These were night riders. The roundup day crew had rolled out about dawn, eaten breakfast, caught and saddled their horses and rode out for the day's work. The night riders then came into camp, took care of their horses, ate breakfast and went to bed.

There was no padding, only a canvas, spread out on the ground and the ground was hard. The man had probably just removed his shirt, trousers and boots and slept in his long johns and socks.

In wet weather, even though they had tents, it was almost impossible to keep the bedding dry.

27

Two cowboys each from a different outfit were bragging about their best bronc rider. The first said that one of their riders could roll a Bull Durham cigarette while riding the bucking bronc.

The second man said that one of their cowboys mounted his bronc with a plate of food and when the horse started to buck he began calmly to eat his lunch. The bronc turned his head around and saw the rider eating lunch, he knew it was no use bucking anymore and just gave up.

The men usually amused themselves by playing practical jokes on one another. One trick was to put a cocklebur under the saddle blanket, when the rider mounted his horse the bucking would start and usually continue until the rider was thrown.

Cowboys have been known to train a horse not to cross a bridge and then sell it to an unsuspecting buyer. The horse was perfectly obedient until it came to a bridge. Then there was no way the rider could get the horse to cross the bridge.

A rope was occasionally slipped into a bed roll in such a way that it felt like a snake when pulled, which usually happened just as the unsuspecting cowboy was about to drop off into sleep. This generally resulted in the bed exploding with the man coming out of it and turning the camp blue with a string of curses.

Young ranch horses that had been running on the range had to be broken for riding when needed and there were men who did this as a specialty, normally charging $5 a head. It was a dangerous occupation. These horses were usually wild mustangs and could bite, kick, and strike out with their front hooves.

There would be criticism of their methods today, but the horses were broken as quickly as possible. The usual method was to use a quirt, a small riding whip. When the horse bucked, the rider laid on the quirt, so the horse soon learned that to buck meant pain. After the horse was broken, the training began. There were three classes of working horses. One was the cowpony, which was used for general work on the ranch and during roundup. The rope horses were trained to stop as soon as an animal was roped and then to keep the rope taut without dragging the captured animal. The highly trained cutting horse would drive a selected animal out of the herd and keep it from getting back. This required extreme ability because the animal being cut would do its best to dodge the horse and get back into the herd. No matter which way the animal turned, the horse had to be just as quick. Sometimes the horse would bite the animal on the rump to drive it away from the herd. The rider, too, had to be on his toes or he might find himself going one direction while the horse was going another.

When the outfit needed more horses, the young stock which had been running freely on the range had to be rounded up and broken.

"Drying beds."

Drying beds.

When the sun was hot a canvas could be stretched for shade.

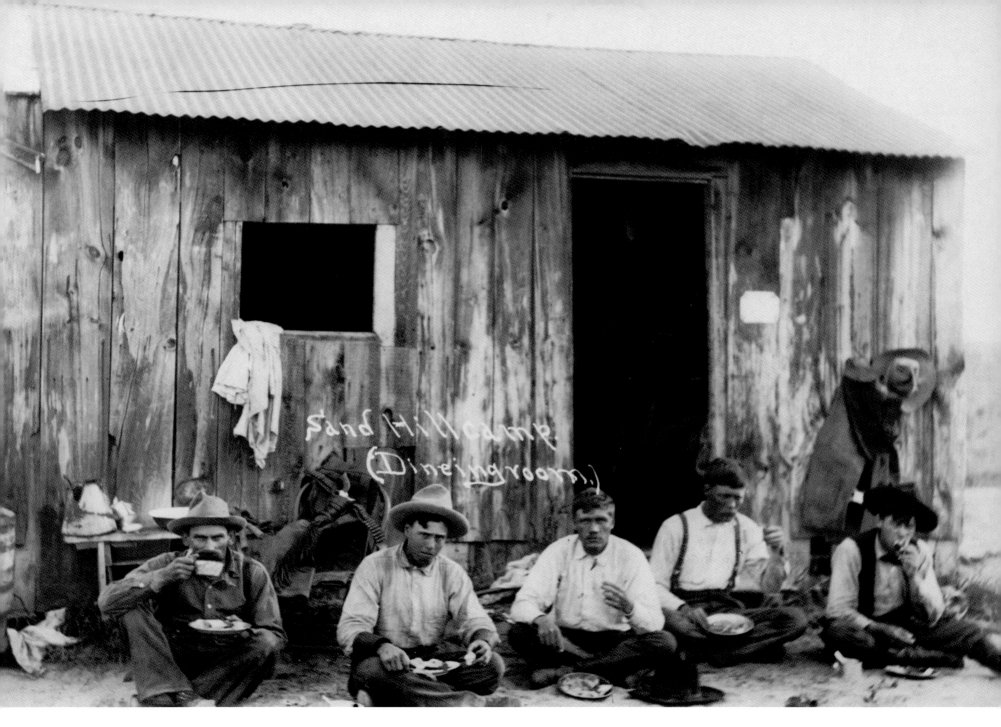

"Sand Hill camp (Dining room)." Near Boyers, Colorado.

"Cow-cooks range & kitchen."

"Our cook can't be beat." One of the most important men on the roundup was the cook. Without good food the men would go and work for another outfit that had a good cook. How many modern cooks could put out a good meal for thirty hungry men from a box and table on the back of a wagon and cook it in large kettles over a fire out in the open?

33

"Sack of Buffalo Chips." There were times when the camp was far from trees or wood and it was necessary to burn dried dung, referred to as "buffalo chips" or "cow chips".

"Grinding coffee."

"Cooking."

"Waiting for dinner."

"The dining room."

"The dining room."

"Cow-boys dining table."

"Cow-boys dining table."

"Help yourself."

"Chuck."

"Chuck."

"Hot biscuit & steak."

"Lady visitors."

"Lady visitors."

48

"Under a cotton-wood tree."

"Get a plate stranger." One story told by the cowboys involved a stranger in camp. The men were dipping cattle when a really tough stranger with a six shooter on each hip came riding up on a grizzly bear. "Howdy fellers," he said. "My horse went lame and I had to shoot him, so I roped a grizzly and broke him to ride. Now I sure am thirsty. Got anything to drink?"

"Sorry but the only thing wet around here is the dip."

The stranger took his hat, filled it up with dip and drank it down. Then he said, "Sorry to drink and run, but there is a tough old Texan after me."

"Noon 'Buffalo Basin.'"

"Waiting for the horses."

"Stay with her boss."

"Suppose he'll buck?"

"He is going to buck." Notice the photographer's shadow in the foreground.

"Practicing."

"Hang on Bill."

"Boss has troubles."

"We have you Mr. Broncho."

"Trimming a broncho's feet."

"Saddling."

"Mounted."

"Starting to work." Lightning was always a threat to a man mounted on a horse. On the treeless plains he is the highest object. There have been riders struck with lightning, which killed both horse and rider.

"Roping horses."

"Just rounded-up

"The day herd."

"A cut for inspection."

"Inspecting a brand."

"Inspecting a brand." There were no fences between ranches and cattle from different ranches ran together. At the roundup these were separated and returned to the proper ranch according to the brand.

"Consulting."

When branding there were certain men to do the job. The iron had to be just the right temperature and held on the animal's hide just the right amount of time. Too long and it burned too deeply, not long enough and the burn could not form a scab that would peel, and the hair would grow back so that the brand would not show.

The man standing with the knife in his hand has the job of castrating the bull calf after it is branded.

"That iron is hot."

"Branding a yearling."

Branding a yearling.

Dipping. The cattle were driven through a deep chute with dip deep enough so that at one place the animals would have to swim. Men were standing at the side to push their heads under so that the entire animal was submerged. The cattle were then held in a draining pen to allow the dip to drain off and run back into the chute. This was to kill the lice and grubs. It would also keep the flies off for some time.

"Draining pen."

"Raising cattle." Occasionally a sick animal could not get up by itself. If it was left alone it would die, but often it could be saved by getting it to its feet. This was usually called *"tailing"* an animal, because it was raised by the tail.

81

"Sand."

"Sand."

"A sand pile."

"A blow out."

"A blow out." At one time this was probably a sandy knoll, then the wind started blowing the sand, eventually leaving a large depression or "blow out."

"All packed."

"Take our picture Mr."

"Let it come."

"Let it come."

"Throw it back there."

"Moveing".

"Moving."

"Unhitching."

The ranch.

"Triplets."

A Time of Change

The late 1800s and early 1900s were a time of change for the area of the United States from Texas to the Canadian border and from the Rocky Mountains to the Missouri River. This had been Indian and buffalo country but the buffalo had been killed and the Indians driven to the reservations by the late 1800s. The country was then opened up for homesteads by the Homestead Act of 1862, which granted land to settlers in one of two ways. One was to prove up on 160 acres and plow and cultivate, at least ten acres and live on the homestead a minimum of five years. The other was to live on the homestead for six months and then pay $1.25 per acre or $200 for title to 160 acres. Some ranches filed claims on land where there was water and hired employees to file on nearby land with water. After six months, the rancher would pay the $200 for a quit claim deed to the land. By owning the land with water, the rancher had control of the land in between.

These earlier inventions made it possible for the homesteaders to farm their land and led to the end of the open range. The first was the invention of the steel moldboard plow which made it possible to plow up the sod. The second was barbed wire. The farmer could fence his property, thereby keeping livestock from trampling his crops. This led to range wars between ranchers and homesteaders in some areas. In this part of Colorado, the transition was relatively peaceful.

In other areas the cattlemen would not tolerate sheep on their range because the sheep ate the grass so close to the ground, there was nothing left for the cattle. On top of the Big Horn mountains in Wyoming, there is a large area which has hills, valleys and large meadows. A long drift fence, running from north to south down the center of the area, separates the sheep range on the west and cattle on the east.

In eastern Oregon around the turn of the century, ranchers organized "The Crook County Sheep Shooters Association." However, in eastern Colorado, many of the ranchers had flocks of sheep as well as cattle.

The third great invention for the farmer was the grain binder which cut and bound the grain into bundles. At that time, it was pulled by four or five horses. The power was supplied by a large wheel under the main part of the binder, called the "bull wheel." The bundles dropped into a carrier which then were dumped into rows.

"Freak lamb."

The shocking was usually done by the wife and children. They leaned the two bundles together with the heads up and continued to add more bundles against these first two until the shock was three or four feet in diameter. The shocking was either done by hand or with a three-tined bundle fork.

Watermelons and Cantaloupes

Ready for Watermelon Day.

Among the pictures Frank Sherman left behind are these views of Watermelon Day. The story comes to us from Ralph C. Taylor's Colorado: South of the Border *(Sage Books, Denver), which is the source of the following.*

With the arrival of the Sante Fe Railroad, new towns and enterprises sprang up in eastern Colorado. One of the pioneers was George W. Swink, who founded the town of Rocky Ford, and established a trading post there with a man named Russell.

Swink had a deep interest in agriculture. While he had been told that nothing would grow in the Arkansas Valley, he persevered and found that with proper irrigation and cultivation a wide range of crops could be raised. He developed varieties of vegetables, grains and hays that would do well in the area.

Taylor reports that "Herbert J. Gardner, who was governor of Massachusetts from 1885-88, sent watermelon and cantaloupe seeds to his homesick son, Herbert, who had settled on the upper Huerfano near the town named for him. Swink obtained some of these seeds and started Colorado's famous melon business.

"The 1878 Swink harvest was bountiful, especially the watermelons. He hauled a wagonload to the railroad station and invited 25 neighbors to a melon feast. He made it an annual affair—the first of Colorado's many and varied harvest festivals."

For a decade Swink produced all of Colorado's cantaloupes and melons. In 1888 his neighbors joined in the production and co-hosted Watermelon Day. The railroad ran special trains to the event, and by 1891 the crowd reached 8,000, and the melon pile was moved to a cottonwood grove at the edge of Rocky Ford.

Watermelon Day continued to grow. In 1895, 20,000 visitors came, and the railroad used 75 passenger cars to meet the demand.

In 1904, after 32 years of experimentation, Swink developed the Rocky Ford Gem Cantaloupe that had a "netted exterior and a salmon or gold flesh." This was introduced about the time that Frank Sherman took the pictures of Watermelon Day.

According to Taylor, Rocky Ford produces relatively few melons today. The Arkansas Valley, however, produces 80 percent of the world's cantaloupe and cucumber seed.

Stanford Sherman against a sod house.

An afternoon hike.

John and Marjorie Eggen.

About the Author

John Eggen was born on a homestead 22 miles northwest of Philip in western South Dakota, April 11, 1912. His parents were Martin and Julia Eggen. John attended a one room school, riding a horse or walking the mile and a half to school, and sometimes arriving at school with frostbitten cheeks or ears in the winter. In the summer he had to herd cattle on the open range when he was big enought to ride a horse. He was expected to grow up to be a farmer. After graduating from the eighth grade, he was sent to the South Dakota School of Agriculture at Brookings, South Dakota. The school term was from October 15th to March 15th. This was to allow the farm boys to finish the fall work and be home in time for spring planting. However, it meant attending class eight hours a day, and four hours on Saturday. Ali the studying was done in the evening.

After graduating, John helped his father on the farm and neighboring ranchers.

John's sister, Margaret, and her husband were ranchers at Dayton, Wyoming. Sometimes after the fall work was done, John would drive out to his sister's ranch and help with the roundup in the foothills of the Big Horn Mountains, occasionally staying for the winter work on the ranch. There were times when he had to spend up to twelve hours in a day on a horse.

The 1930s became known as the "Dirty Thirties" because of drought, dust storms, grasshoppers, and low prices for cattle and grain.

By 1938, John had acquired 720 acres of owned and rented land. Then, in early 1939, John had the misfortune of permanently injuring his back while playing hockey with a group of farm men and boys. This ended his farming career. In April of 1941 John drove to Los Angeles, taking four other young men with him to work in the Aircraft Industry. John was given a job in the Photo Department of Lockheed Aircraft because he had some prior photographic experience while staying with his brother Ray in Detroit, Michigan.

In April 1941, John and his longtime sweetheart, a South Dakota school teacher, Marjorie Olson were married in Our Saviour's Lutheran Church in Los Angeles. While living in Los Angeles John and Marjorie attended night school at the Art Center, and took a course in photography, one of the instructors was the famous photographer Ansel Adams.

In July, 1945, John gave up his job a Lockheed, and Marjorie and he returned to South Dakota so John could help his father with the wheat harvest as there was no other help to be had as the war had just ended.

In November of that year John and Marjorie drove to Lebanon, Oregon to visit friends and found a studio there for sale. They purchased it and operated a photography business until 1977 when they sold out and retired.

In 1967 John was elected President of the Professional Photographers of Oregon and in 1968 he was elected Mayor of Lebanon for the years 1969-1970.

About 1966 John was offered some boxes of glass negatives—over three hundred of them. The woman who called the studio told him that if he didn't want them she was going to take them to the Lebanon dump. John picked them up—published two editions of "The West that Was" which portrayed the life of the cowboys around the turn of the century. Cowboys is the final product from these beautiful glass negatives.